They
Resilient

Kristen Quinn

BookLeaf
Publishing

Presentation by *BookLeaf Publishing*

Web: www.bookleafpub.com

E-mail: info@bookleafpub.com

ISBN: 9789357617697

First edition 2022

This book is dedicated, with great reluctance, to my mother, because she forced me to. Just kidding.

Personally, I would have liked to have included my best friend Kristyn who has stuck by my side for the last 10 years but I felt that might be too corny.

I wish I had room to mention my dear friend Maxim who fights my battles with me, but sadly there was a character limit, sorry max.

21 things about turning 21

21- It's expected that you drink an alcoholic beverage. A beverage that will change your behavior. A beverage to make you happy.

20- You're expected to be happy.

19- You're as adult as much as the definition can stretch. Too old to pawn off bad behavior as immaturity, too young to do anything great without luck.

17- With some luck I won't have a hangover tomorrow. I heard that's a sign that you had a good night, and good friends, and a good time?

16- You can buy your own drinks now, it's so expensive to replicate your birthday night, to chug a few beers in hopes that the percentage of alcohol will do more than any self-care bubble bath could.

15- All I can think about is the BAC, ABV, congeners, units per hour, 80 proof, alcohol poisoning.

15- Did I already do 15? My new favorite is a can of wine, quite the invention. I can drink a can in two minutes and get the effects of 2.5 glasses. When you're having dark thoughts it takes the cake for first responder.

14-

13-

11- Chemical imbalances are coming back in season and the only chemical I've found that makes me feel less is now something I have to hide.

10- This has become quite the list. Depression sucks, and the one coping skill I've found to work can and will and might already have turned into an addiction.

8- Can a coping skill be an addiction or should it be referred to as a saving grace with a touch of dangerous potential?

7-

5- Fuck this list. The only list I'm interested in is the menu at the bar i'm headed to. I hope they have a good burger.

3-

2-They don't tell you that after a few good beers and a little mental illness, you've been involuntarily subscribed to an overpriced concoction of never having to deal with your feelings again. Trading everything that was once important to you, for another bottle of bourbon.

1- Think it's time for another beer.

Moving on

I want a panoramic view of your perspective
I tattooed the pain you caused
Onto the back of my eyelids
As a reminder
So that every time I wake up
I know I'm better off without you

This room of mine

I trust my room more than anyone.
The blinds didn't flicker shut
when I shared my fears of failing.
The door didn't close in my face
when I threatened to slam it.
The wall didn't crumble before me
when I curled against it to cry.
The floorboards continue to hold me
even when I etch my insecurities into the grain.
The ceiling didn't collapse on me
when I continued yelling to a god above.
So when I share with you,
will you last longer than this room of mine?

My cure needs a refill

They give you a bottle of pills
They say take one a day
Sorta like an apple a day keeps the doctor away
They don't tell you what to do when you feel
dead
Before your funeral
You're stuck at the crime scene to-be
Wondering if its worth it
You go home, just push it off till tomorrow
But too many a day and you just end up
ordinarily dead
You want to unlike yourself in a parallel reality
Just so you can see and hope and realize that the
people around you
Really do want you to stay
To try on different scenarios of your life like
costumes, but
None quite fit right
Apologize to my brain for wanting to move
away
You want this grand solution to your
monumental pain
Yet the 60 minutes of discussing it just seems
too short
The dosage too low

1 a day feels like the 3-in-1 shampoo
Where it just doesn't quite cut it
And sometimes you do want to cut
Not because it's an addiction but
The pain it causes can drown out the static in
your brain
You just need to be careful not to turn it too loud

Silas laughed as he fell

He watched as the skyscrapers rose above him
and
peacefully waited for Mother Nature to
give him that hug, a hug
he had waited for over 20 years for

Silas knew there would be a night to come
Where the pages of his diary would be sewn
together to
Form his coffin
But he did not know that his words
Were to be left in the nearby pond
For another little warrior to find.

Silas' only want, was to fly
To fly above the acidic lake that would birth
His worst nightmares
To soar past the worries that he'd never
Be good enough, for anyone even himself

To victoriously smile down at the battles of the
past as
If they were minuscule compared to today

Silas had wrote, that pain was never meaningless

But he also wrote,
A beer a day keeps the doctor in layaway

Silas loved airplanes, he wanted to be a pilot
He was enrolled in an aviation program, to start
next fall
He knew he loved to fly, even though his feet
had been
Chained down to the core of this earth, he knew

He knew a lot, he also knew that some planes
had to
Land in cornfields and oceans
He knew those planes still served a purpose

Silas jumped today
He was not broken or tired, he was calm
He completed the last war that was projected to
last a lifetime
He was victorious
Silas won

Coping

I cry the hardest
When no one is there to be a witness
To provide an alibi when the words
'How are you- I'm fine' are spoken
To just hold me while
The ocean falls from my eyes
Physical comfort to actually comfort
Instead it's a trigger to my trauma
When the touch wasn't to comfort
Instead brings exhaustion
I sleep then repeat

Unfinished

It's been 8 hours and 218 days since
I've seen you
I saw the TV share the graphics before I got the
call
My neighbors knew before I
In my dreams I still hear your voice cheering me
on
To keep fighting my battles
These thoughts might take me but three bullets
took you first
Your body was a crime scene to be meticulously
prodded at
So when I saw your face one last time
No makeup was applied
The shadow framed your face so well
I thought perhaps you never lived
You were the one to say go for it when I was
facing
Mountainous challenges
Now I face the edge of a tall building
Your face only an echo
What's life but the people around us
And when the people aren't around us
What's life
There was only a comma left over the sentence
was,

Sudden goodbyes

There is an ending to every story
But yours came too soon
When the time came to say hi
I passed by thinking I was, too busy
When the time came by to talk about your TV
show
I passed by thinking I was, too tired
I'm sorry I wasn't there
I'm sorry you didn't see me as a bearing wall
I'm sorry that your pain went
Unseen, unshared, too overwhelming to tackle
It may not mean much, but I'm here
I'm here in shock that your ending wasn't
A beginning
A beginning is all there is left to have
So I will begin to learn from my mistakes
I will learn from your strength and hurt
I will learn to be a better friend
I'll be a better friend because of you

Pain hides in heels

I'm running away but I seem to never get close enough
To the finish line
The line that I drew, when I still had hope
Every two steps I take, the line moves five
What will it take for the pain to leave
Just to be felt then discarded
She cuts six inches deep but never draws blood
How will anyone see her abuse when
There are no scars to be found
Will anyone see me drowning if I still manage to take a breath
I keep walking here and there
But I don't manage to go anywhere
There are days when she tricks me
Into thinking that there is a reason
To keep going, to keep trying, to fight back
But today isn't one of them
Today I sit with the monsters that I've created
I think, has she already won
What if, What if
I can
Hold onto my ration of hope
Could I, attempt the climb knowing I may fail
Uncertainty lies ahead, am I willing to take

A step, with only a lamp's light to guide my way
I don't know if I can fight anymore
What will happen when everyone finds out, that
in this square world I've managed to be
shapeless
I can fit in when needed, when I show only one
side
But if someone see's the whole me
They'll know I've been a fraud, all along
I want to be free
I can't figure out the answer, do I give into her
and say goodbye
Or do I search for the strength to keep living
She demands to be felt, I just wish
That there is some meaning to this race
Will I reach the finish line

Create the key

I carry the shame in my back pocket
These voices in my head say "give up"
My doctors say you're fine just take your pills
My friends say you're strong just keep going
I say, I can't do this much longer

You'd never know I stopped fighting 17 days ago
I had given up and given in
A few dozen pills later and the hospital bed
The only thing holding me up
I shut the door to my mind and pulled the blinds
shut
For fear the sun would emerge and reawaken
My desire to live
The inside of my head was a cage I was locked
in
The key, yet to be created

Dancing my way through

My tears fall like rain to form an ocean
Never seen, so no name given to acknowledge
their existence
The waves invisible due to the isolation being
more
consistent than any concerned advice you could
ever give
The monsters on the ocean floor live with more
detail
than any of my childhood nightmares
The water so frigid, shivered rattle my skeleton
like a maraca
The rhythm ungracefully bashing my eardrums
I can still dance my way through public
as if i'm a functioning human being
My thoughts swimming through my brain like
alphabet soup
the only ones within grasp are the P, T, S, and D
My tears fall like rain to form an ocean

In the moment

Breathe in, Breathe out
I wish I had air to fill my lungs
even more than the current second,
but alas
I'm not promised any more than the present.
Feeling down because the present
doesn't feel like a present,
Maybe I'm just missing the ribbon and bow?
Breathe in, breathe out
I trust that oxygen will find its way
to my lungs, to further display
that I can do without
A ribbon and bow.
You'll just have to settle for the natural glow.

12:54 AM

I try to hold all of the masks on
But, I stumble
I drop a few, feeling more exposed than ever
Do I have a real face underneath all these?
Change my name, my hair, my smile
My thoughts, beliefs
Just to keep up with the facade
Lost count of the passing days, years
I frantically grasp for a mask
One that will allow me to, fit in
To feel included, to be the, same
Lest someone find out the truth
I've been a fraud all along.
I take a glance at those around me
Hlf-smiles, eye bags prevalent
T-shirts proclaiming "only good vibes"
I wonder, how many masks do they hide under?
Masks forced to peel away
Two by three by five
A few too many
This is not ok
I can't stand this
Feeling, so bare
I guess I'll just create another one.

Retail therapy

I see the boy running
He's running with his copy of
The lion king, held tightly to his chest
as if it's his most cherished treasure.
He looks so happy even when some pages are
Missing, so satisfied with the torn cover
He appreciates the words it holds.
I'm struck by how simple it looks
How his happiness doesn't rely on
Many possessions.
All I can think about is the
Daily retail therapy I take part in
The many possessions I look at
But never have time to enjoy since I'm
Still searching.
Searching for something I know
The books and puzzles won't give me.
Yet I still shop as if the money transaction
Will give me credit that will transfer
To my brain as satisfaction.
The kind that
You can only see as a boy running with a single
book
That he'd even give away if it meant
Another could share in the happiness he has.
Perhaps, I have it all wrong.

Refurbished

I have a theory that I was made with broken
parts.
You could say refurbished, I'd say
Still not in working condition.
See this brain I have,
the chemicals have over mixed.
See these thoughts I have
have overstepped.
See this life I have
has been overlived.
I think my heart is heavier than the scale can
handle
And my mind is too dark for the pictures to
capture.
See my life is a sentence and all I have left is a
period.
I just don't know how this one will end.

Is self-love possible?

Sure, I compare myself to others
I can think that someone is funnier than me
That someone is happier
    or taller or prettier, skinnier, faster
        or smarter, or ...anything
But there is still one thing they don't have
My combination.
The combination of characteristics that makes
me, me!
Nobody can take that away from me,
This isn't a trade-up situation
It's not the characteristics I have that
make me better than another
That's not the goal.
There's no measuring tool.
What matters is the way I use my talents
and since there is no measuring stick,
doesn't that mean that there isn't a grading
system?
And if that's the case, I'm not failing, and if I'm
not failing
I think I'd rather spend my time
Loving myself then searching for reasons why I
shouldn't.
So, the self-love doesn't start when

I get the job I want, or clean my room
at the start of a relationship, or when someone
praises me.
It starts now. Regardless of anything.
Because self-love isn't attained by anything
Other than what already exists inside of me.

The cost of my attention

Your cup is overflowing with my love
Yet mine seems to have only caught a few
droplets.
when will it rain? Will it?
I know that even though I've given you myself
I cannot love you into loving me, back.
I have the honor of scrolling through your
smiles,
Do you see mine?
I wouldn't spare a second to choose you in this
lifetime
But I see no votes for me in your eyes.
I can survive on just the droplets, for now.
But they don't quench the thirst.
I just wish that for once, the weight of the fear
Of losing me
Would make the scale notch, twitch, just a little.

Unrequited love

Some might say the most painful kind of love.
I've fallen in love with you
In my mind, through the tunnels of fantasy.
I made the jump over the nonexistent cliff
Only to look back and see, you never did.
Since this began I've suffered only in languages
no one speaks.

Eating a cup of applesauce with a fork because I
haven't done dishes in a week
Eating a cup of applesauce to cover up the
hunger pains from not eating enough
Eating a cup of applesauce since its within reach
of my bed
Eating a cup of applesauce, its the only thing I
have enough energy to do

You'd think I was going through a breakup
Yet there's never been anything to break
Except the hope I misplaced in a reality
That'll never exist outside of my mind.

Puzzle box

My family is like a shaken box of puzzle pieces.
My mom is the center piece,
holding us together.
My sister is a missing piece,
that lost its way.
My father is the piece that just won't fit,
no matter where you try
My grandma, she's the edges,
protecting us.
My brother is the piece that connects us together.
And me, I'm the broken box trying to hold us all
together.

Would you recognize my name?

When I came into this world
My father dug a 5 ft. deep hole and kindly
placed me in it.

I stare up at the sky in peaceful oblivion
Not yet realizing I'd need to pull myself out to
start living.
Covered in dirt as if, I was the problem.
To be buried with no intention of a eulogy.
Our only connection
The bank account receiving your monthly
contributions in the form of
Burial insurance, deposited to support me.
It was never enough.

At 9 years old, was finally old enough to
understand.
That you had made your choice. And the
anguish was deafening
When I realized, it wasn't me.

If you stayed
Would you have protected me?

From the lasting scars left by the ghosts vying
for your place
The perpetual memories of abuse felt
Like dirt mixing into my bloodstream.
I wanted to lay down in that hole again.
Growing up, men would come and go
Filling up the hole with trinkets and bobbles
None willing to stay to clean off the very
skeletons they try to cover.
I'd venture off to school and daydream about
the scenarios of how I might react if you had the
audacity to come, but
Still wanting you to
To prove you might still care
And feeling dejected knowing you, won't.

The therapist said:
It is worse to have and to have lost,
I say:
It is worse to not have and feel lost
With no expiration date to the pain.
This isn't a cliffhanger from a movie, leaving
you, moldy dissatisfied.
It's like repeatedly uncovering wounds before
they can heal.
Mixing in more dirt until no shower can make
you feel clean.

Father's Day can be heart rending.

Teachers would pass out sheets of thick
construction paper.
Expecting us to fill it with the weight of our love
for "daddy".
Even saying   daddy Feels like a foreign object
trailing through my intestines.
Yet in this cacophony of crayon all I can see is
Condolence cards littering the funeral home
Iv'e grown up in.
I would just sit,
Not knowing what I should write
Other than the hurt and unanswered questions,
but
You buried those answers when you left.

If you stayed
I wouldn't have the burden of preparing for a
funeral of a mother
whose life has yet to be taken.
Having to get a degree not for me, but to keep a
roof over us,
Wanting to create art, but having difficulty
choosing
Whether to get more pencils or replace my dirty
hole-ridden shoes.
I wouldn't have to share that I don't have a dad
Just to accept the flowers and sympathy cards.
Then pretend to be ok,   and say its ok,   and
convince everyone

That I'm ok
But it's not ok,
I'm not ok!

I've learned to cope, in a way.
Throughout my time here on this earth.
At school, I've looked for ghosts but only found
the midnight cats
Sneaking into my grave, to leave by dawn.
I've been filling the grave with the wrong bodies.
I'd spend my time with some of my teachers,
Or coaches, or principal, or- stranger.
Sometimes asking questions I already
Knew the answers to.
I was continuously on E and searching for any
male role-model
Who'd give me some attention, a refill.
Secretly pretending they were my father.
Showing me how to throw a football,
Answering the difficult questions,
Helping me with homework.
I continuously strove to be the best at everything
I tried.
When my teacher would say, "here's your A"
It felt like a father saying, "that's my girl, good
job".

It felt like coping, but I only gained a minute
sense of control.

By picking up the shovel that once dug that hole.
Covering up my skeleton with dirt.

I was devastated when I came to know
You left when I was born, I suppose you thought
closing me in the
Casket would
Give you a fresh start, but you didn't even lock
it, you Coward.
You have a family of your own.
My existence   the only threat to your 'good life'.

If you stayed
We wouldn't have driven around looking to the
ground for \
Quarters, to wash the dirt off our clothes.
Perhaps we could have had a family vacation
like, other families.
Like my peers at school during summer,
Kinda hard to answer the back-to-school
question of-
"where did ya go this summer?"
The kids who went to Florida,
Always receiving the greatest applause.
I don't even know the capital of Florida.
No, Dad's gotta earn the bread for 'his' family.
Once again, left in the dirt.

There is no happy ending.

You made sure of that.
The child-support coming in
The only indication of your continued existence.
Now that's gone too.

All I'm left with is the reeling sense of
disorientation.
Like I'm back in that hole you dug, and I can't
get   out.
You could be living in your daydream.
Your most significant worry, burning your tea.
This anger etching at me every night,
Slowly engraving my hate, permanently into
your fantastical identity.
With no certainty if you're even alive.
Sometimes I forget your name.
Shame crowds inside me.

Do you know mine?

Today I have power

A few years ago, I would have considered this
day to be
one of the worst days of my life.

The worst days of your life are supposed to be a
messy bun,
tears streaming down, snot on your sleeves kind
of day.

Today's not that kind of day because today is a
day where
some of the strength inside of me was realized.

When I realized that I survived, I told myself
that this
must be evidence of growth.

I've grown into a strong woman.
A powerfully empowering powerful woman.

I wasn't a powerful woman when the clothes
were
indelicately removed without my permission.

In addition, I am not a victim anymore.

A few years ago, I would have considered the thought
of ever seeing your face again, like today, to be
a reminder of my place.

A place where I succumb to the thoughts of being
lesser, of being less of a human than you.

My place, a place where I exist in my own strength,
and your name is not listed in the credits.

Printed in the USA
CPSIA information can be obtained
at www.ICGtesting.com
LVHW020923061023
760263LV00038B/970